Counting the Days…The Break up Guide

By
J. Bohn

PublishAmerica
Baltimore

First printing

This publication contains the opinions and ideas of its author. Author intends to offer information of a general nature. Any reliance on the information herein is at the reader's own discretion.

The author and publisher specifically disclaim all responsibility for any liability, loss, or right, personal or otherwise, which is incurred as a consequence, directly or indirectly, of the use and application of any contents of this book. They further make no representations or warranties with respect to the accuracy or completeness of the contents of this work and specifically disclaim all warranties including without limitation any implied warranty of fitness for a particular purpose. Any recommendations are made without any guarantee on the part of the author or the publisher.

PublishAmerica has allowed this work to remain exactly as the author intended, verbatim, without editorial input.

Hardcover 978-1-4512-2282-1
Softcover 978-1-4512-2283-8
PUBLISHED BY PUBLISHAMERICA, LLLP
www.publishamerica.com
Baltimore

Printed in the United States of America

Forward

Breakups
They can be ecstatic,
or they can be dramatic.
and even terribly traumatic.
Some will bring you down,
make you want to wear a frown,
or even make you want to drown.
Some of them are happy!
Some of them are sappy,
some will have you feeling mean, unclean,
and genuinely crappy
Some can make you glad!
While others make you sad,
and sometimes even mad, or bad,
or feeling like a total cad.
They can make you broke,
or make you want to choke, or smoke,
or make you feel as though your life,
is nothing but a joke.
Breakups can be mischievous,
or devious,
or make you feel the ways that have, herein,
been mentioned previous.
Breakups make us cry,
and sigh,
and often lie,
or even make us want to die—
these strange, strange ways we have
for simply saying: '*bye.*'

So I'm cuddling with my sweetheart one evening many, many years ago. We'd just had some of the most awe-inspiring sex known to the human race. And the phone rings. I'm a gentleman, of course, so I let the machine pick up, rather than disturb the quality time I'm enjoying with the new love of my life.

"Hi, darling," I hear from the answering machine. "It's me. I'm right down the street and thought I'd pop in. Hope you're there. I'll see you in a few. Love you!" Click.

Uh-oh.

Okay, okay, so I had more than one sweetheart. Anybody whose read my previous book, *Off the Slope: The Cheater's Guide to Romance*, probably already knows that. But hey, that was the old me. I'm a one-at-a-time guy now. And in truth, I had planned on being a one-at-a-time guy then, too. The problem was, I just hadn't gotten around to breaking things off with the woman who was, as that very moment, on her way to see me.

I found myself in a panic. I wasn't so much worried about her finding out I was cheating. After all, I was going to break up with her anyway. It's just that the breakup would have to come now, rather than later, rather than when I was more prepared. Oh sure, I could have told my new love to hide in the closet, but I knew that that would only delay the inevitable. (I also knew she'd probably slap me if I suggested the closet thing.)

I found myself counting the minutes. I had maybe five to consider what I was going to say, rehearse it, and polish it. We'd been going out for awhile. We had been intimate. We had told each other, "I love you." This was nothing that could be done brusquely. This needed to be handled delicately, and with finesse and tact.

Four minutes went by. I had nothing.

Then there was a light tap on the door. I opened it. "It's over, babe," I said. And I closed the door in her face. It was quite possibly the worst (non-violent) breakup of all times, but it was all I could think of. Of course it didn't end there. She knocked again and I opened the door again. She saw my new lover behind me wearing nothing but one of my dress shirts. We talked some more. Okay, she actually screamed. And

I still got my face slapped. Worse, she refused to come to grips with the situation, actually dragging out the breakup over the course of the next several days with numerous phone calls, each one uglier than the one before.

Counting the minutes that night was one of the worst experiences of my life. And I vowed that the next time I was ready to break up with a woman, I would be prepared. I would never count minutes. I would count the days. I would pick an actual "breakup date" sometime in the near future—maybe a month and no more—and I would count the days instead.

There are good breakups and there are bad breakups and the difference is twofold: preparation and commitment. A breakup is an unexploded shell. If you don't handle it just right, it's going to blow up in your face. But if you treat it with respect and handle it gently, you might just be able to walk away in one piece.

Since that awkward, ugly night, I have made a study of breaking up. In these pages you will find the keys that will allow you to deal with any breakup situation with the grace and tact that eluded me that fateful night, even ones where you're on the other side, counting the days until your significant other breaks up with you.

Look, no matter what side you're on, it's all about inevitability. Chances are good that somewhere along the line, one way or the other, you're going to be involved in a serious breakup. I can't stop that from happening, but maybe I can make it go a little smoother.

SECTION ONE
So You Want to Break Up

ONE
Are You *Sure* You Want to Break Up?

"Are you sure you want to break up" is the question that must be asked before you go even one more step. Have you really thought this through? It might be the best idea you've ever had, or it might end up being your worst. The stakes are high. Let's examine all the reasons for breaking up. Let's shine the cold light of reason on them, one at a time, and see what they really look like. Some are better than others. Yours is in here somewhere. Do you recognize it? And is it good enough?

Happy, or not happy? Unhappiness is a pretty damn good reason. Does your significant other make you feel like a little kid on Christmas morning when he or she comes into the room? Is he or she your very favorite person *in the world?* Or, are you finding yourself feeling ambivalent when your significant other is around. Or worse…

Are you ashamed of your significant other? Are you purposely keeping this person away from your friends and family? If so it's time to break up. In fact, it's probably past time. Finish this book and go do it.

What about age? Age differences can be real deal-breakers. Everybody seems to deny this. "Age is just a number," they say. So is "666" but I wouldn't want to see it tattooed on my dentist's scalp. Is your significant other so young that they should be wearing diapers? Is your significant other so *old* they should be wearing diapers? Think long-term. What's this relationship going to look like in ten or twenty years?

Sex. Is it good enough? Is it mind-blowing? Is it at least memorable? Sex is 60% of a relationship. People think money is the chief cause of problems between two people. Nope. It's sex. If somebody's not satisfied, that somebody becomes a very likely candidate to cheat.

The little things. That little way he has of clearing his throat all the time. The adorable way she has of always asking questions throughout the whole movie. Can you live with these things the rest of your life? They're cute and quirky at first. But quirky can become annoying practically overnight. When that happens, the little things become *big* things.

Parallel interests. Opposites attract. Maybe. But likenesses endure. Look at your hobbies, style of clothing, food preferences. If he likes rap and she likes country, it won't work. Ever. Look at your body types. Are you ripped and lean and she's plump and flabby? Are you skinny and tall and he's short and squat? When you stand next to each other in public do people think of the number 10?

Religion. Can a Christian fundamentalist live happily ever after with an Islamic extremist? (Can anybody live with *either*?) Are you going to be able to peacefully co-exist in December with both a Christmas tree *and* a menorah in the house? Do you fight over which church to go to, or fight about going to church at all?

Cultural/ethnical differences. He's a white Anglo-Saxon Protestant living just outside of Davenport, Iowa. She's a black Yorubo spiritualist originally from the center of Abuja, Nigeria. A beautiful relationship with great potential, or a really terrible idea for a sitcom? You be the judge.

Is somebody looking for a sugar daddy? How important is money to you? How much does he/she have? How much will he/she have in the future? Is that what you're into the relationship for? Are the prospects in line with your expectations? On the other hand, are you beginning to wonder what he or she is looking for from *you*? She's twenty-two and hot. You're fifty-eight and rich. Do I really need to connect the dots for you?

Is it love or lust? Seriously. Have you mistakenly interpreted your lustful desires as love? Don't be ashamed. Happens all the time. It's one of the big causes for divorce, actually, and an easy mistake to make. Take a cold shower and then take some time to think about this one.

Cheating. If you're cheating, that's a pretty good reason to break up. If you're significant other is cheating, that's an even better reason.

Abuse. It doesn't just have to be physical. Are you being mentally abused? Is your significant other verbally controlling? Get out. Now.

Health issues. Hey, look, it's no sin to admit that you don't want to spend your days taking care of somebody or pushing their wheelchair or helping them into (and out of) the bathtub. Does it make you a little small? Well, yes, but you have a right to be happy too.

Weight issues. Can you handle, for the long haul, the fact that your significant other is big and most likely getting even bigger?

Fear of commitment. This one can be good or bad. It takes a big person to admit that he or she just isn't ready for a long-term thing. Then again, you have to ask yourself why that is and what you think will eventually change that for you. You're not getting any younger, you know.

One final note: is your possible break up more serious than the garden-variety one between boyfriend and girlfriend? Are you facing the possibility of divorce? Then the thought you're giving to the matter has to increase one-hundred fold. With financial considerations, residence issues, and possibly children in the mix, yours isn't a break up; yours is a life transition. Take your time.

TWO
Let Me Count the Ways...

Sixteen. That's how many ways there are to break up. Paul Simon sang that there are "fifty ways to leave your lover," but I think he exaggerated. Everything pretty much fits into one of these categories:

The Runaway. It doesn't get any simpler than this. At least at first. You just leave. This is great for cowards or even people who are just too busy to take the time for a proper parting of the ways. The downside, though, is that you leave unfinished business behind and unfinished business can come back to bite you in the ass. Your significant other is going to want some answers and you might be inadvertently creating a stalker.

The voicemail break-up. This requires a little more involvement than the runaway, but not much. You call your significant other when you're sure he or she isn't going to be near their phone. You declare that "it's over" and maybe even list a couple reasons. Then you hang up and you're on your way! It avoids the nasty face-to-face possibilities. Technological variations of this include text-messaging your intentions, or even Twittering them or posting them to your Facebook page. Still, there's just a whiff of cowardice in this method. You'll have to decide if this is the right way for you.

The Dear John letter. This is a classic that goes back millennia. There's no telling who was the first recipient of one of these heartbreaking bombs. (Probably some guy named John.) At any rate, these give you the ability to make sure your thoughts are all in proper order. Today's technological variation is, of course, a Dear John e-mail. Just hope it doesn't get trapped in your significant other's spam folder.

The "It's not You, it's Me." Seinfeld's George Costanza claims to have invented this one, but I suspect it's been around almost as long as the Dear John letter. If you've decided to go through with a face-to-face, this is a pretty decent approach. Just try to make it sound sincere.

The Band-Aid approach. In a face to face encounter it's best to be quick about it, just like pulling off a band-aid. No beating around the bush. Get right to the point, take your punches, and get the hell out of there.

The weeper. It's hard for your significant other to be mad at you or otherwise blame you for breaking up when he or she sees how deeply the breakup is affecting you. A few heartfelt, well-placed sobs during the deed can do wonders to soften the blow. When your significant other starts to say things to comfort *you*, then you know you're doing it right.

The serious, no-nonsense approach. This is good for breakups that have the potential to be explosive and confrontational. If you feel like your significant other is going to hit back with anger and threats, you need to take charge from the very start. Never let 'em see you sweat. Fear can be sensed, and you need to dictate the mood. You need to be strong, certain, and curt. There is no room for equivocation and wishy-washiness here.

The let's-stay-friends approach. This one's been around forever and, yes, it seems clichéd, but only because it works so well. By declaring that you still need your significant other's friendship, you'll be giving him or her some much-needed validation at a very critical moment. Later, of course, you can renege on the whole "friend" idea but it's a damn nice thing to say at the time.

The sexual orientation switcharoo. Breaking up is a great time to come out of the closet. Even if you were never in it. You can't stay with your significant other because you just discovered you're gay! Or, if you're breaking up with your gay significant other, you just discovered you're straight!

The fear of commitment effect. You have to do this one without sounding like a wuss, or he or she will continue to try to help you "overcome" your fear. The timing's just not right, is what you want to emphasize. You have other things going on in your life—career, family troubles, health issues, a serious drug addiction (use your imagination) and you just can't possibly continue with the relationship at this point in time.

The long-distance predicament. You'd love to continue the relationship, but you're moving away. To a strange, faraway land, like Borneo or Timbuktu or Cleveland. Long-distance relationships never work out. Everybody knows this and so you're doing your significant other a favor by breaking up with him or her before you leave.

The Break. This one's less of a commitment to breaking up than a clear break-up like, for example, the Runaway or the Dear John. But it still gets you going in the right direction and perhaps not as painfully for your significant other. Let's just take a break, you offer, so that you can "sort some things out." Then you simply never call him or her ever again.

The Let's Date Other People Maneuver. You want to date other people but you would never dream of doing so behind your significant other's back. That's cheating, after all! And you're not a cheater. So you come clean and tell him or her upfront that you'll be seeing other people. The break-up normally takes care of itself at this point.

The Win-Win. When I was a cop, a routine traffic stop was considered successful if you got the driver to say thank you and shake your hand *after* you handed him the citation. That means you explained the infraction to his satisfaction, you were polite and professional, and your handling of the situation was perfectly diplomatic. If you can keep all of this in mind as your goal in the break-up, you'll have him or her thanking you for the experience of having been with you and telling you that you'll always be fondly remembered. Parting really can be such sweet sorrow!

The blow-up. When in doubt, just explode on 'em. In an angry fit, list all of the things about him or her that you can no longer stand. There. That should do it.

The serve. If there's a divorce involved, and none of these seem quite appropriate, you might want to consider simplifying. Just have the papers served. Easy-peasy.

THREE
Here, There, Everywhere

Where to break up is almost as important as how. Some places are better than others.

The Restaurant. Classic location for a break-up. But be wary of public places if your significant other is prone to angry outbursts. You don't want to get a fork stuck in your head or a cup of hot coffee splashed in your face. Generally speaking, restaurants are best for women breaking up with men. Men are more inclined to try to keep their cool in public. It's part of the guy code: never let anybody see you lose it. But either way, just make sure it's not an expensive place. This is *not* a romantic evening out.

Her house. This is a good one because you can do the deed and then just leave. Some precautions: always stay near the door or at least know where all the emergency exits are. In case of flying dishes you'll need a quick exit strategy. And make sure you grab all your stuff. You don't want to have to go back later.

His house. Not good. He's the king of his castle. No guy likes to be dressed down on his own turf. If you must, take the same precautions as above.

Your house. Good if you're a woman. He'll probably just want to slink out. Bad if you're a guy. She'll be needy and want to stay. Either way, make sure the breakables are all out of sight, and make sure they take all their stuff. If you're sharing a house, have a fair plan in place for who should leave and a plan for where the person can go. Kicking somebody out onto the street just isn't right. (Plus, they'll be less likely to want to leave.)

A parking lot. You meet your significant other at a restaurant and, before you enter, you break up right there in the parking lot. "Before we go in…" you start to say. He or she won't see it coming and sometimes that's the best way to deliver bad news. Then, you both repair to your respective cars and drive off into your respective sunsets. Who's going to feel like dinner after that?

The mall. Again, a public place where it's probably better for a girl breaking up with a guy. He's less apt to explode in anger and, even if he does, there are too many witnesses for you to come to any real bodily harm.

A friend's house. Not when they're there, of course (nobody needs an audience watching as their heart is being ripped out), but sometimes with a neutral yet familiar site, there are less complications.

In the car. Sometimes a break-up happens in the car because the person just can't wait long enough to actually arrive somewhere. It's okay, but there are some precautions that need to be taken. I lost over a hundred CDs breaking up with a girl in the car one time. I imagine people are still finding them scattered along the 405 outside of Los Angeles. (If you come across my Radiohead *OK Computer* CD, let me know. I really miss that one.) The point is, don't have anything within reach that your significant other can toss out the window. And it's best to be going slow, even stopped. A break-up is almost as bad distraction-wise as text messaging. Finally, never break up *as a passenger*—not when your significant other has control of two tons of moving steel.

Airports. There's something poetically appropriate about generating a life-changing transition in a place that exists for the sole purpose of sending people off in different directions. From a practical standpoint, if you're dropping your significant other off at the airport because they're flying out of town for a business trip or to visit relatives somewhere, what better time to break up? You do the deed, guaranteed to soon be geographically removed from them. They might be miserable on the plane, but they'll be *on the plane—*flying *away*.

Out of town. You're both out of town somewhere. Break up and go your separate ways. Do *not* travel home together unless it's your intention to create an entirely new definition for the word "awkward."

FOUR
Timing is Everything

You know why, you know how, you know where. Let's talk about when. Rule number one: make it on *your* terms. You pick the date so you'll be ready. Then count the days till you get there. Some good days to break up, some not-so-good:

A holiday. I once broke up with a girl on Christmas Day. What was I thinking?! The truth is, I just couldn't take it anymore. I couldn't go one more day. And this highlights the importance of having a firm break-up date in mind. If I had been on a well-thought out schedule, I could have survived the day (and kept my Christmas presents).

His or her birthday. This is only a good day if you want to be remembered as a complete asshole for the remainder of your significant other's life, at least on every single one of their ensuing birthdays.

When friends or family are around. Nobody wants to have to suffer a break-up in front of loved ones. Can't you wait until you're alone? Or at least in an anonymous crowd?

Your anniversary. Of when you met, your first date, first kiss, first roll in the hay, whatever. Nothing communicates disrespect quite like the insensitivity of ignoring a relationship milestone, even if the relationship is headed for its demise. Not a good day to break up.

Death in the family. Try to have a little compassion. This is not a good time, needless to say. On the other hand, suppose you've picked a date in the future that subsequently turns out to tragically be the day of someone's funeral. Then what? Judgment call. If it was me? I'd probably continue with the break-up. But that's just the way I roll. When in doubt, I always try to remember this: it's not about them, it's about me.

Health trouble. Your significant other discloses to you that he or she has one year to live. Problem is, you don't want to wait around that long. (Doctors are notoriously wrong—it could take *years*.) Stick with your schedule. It's the one thing you have control over. The break-up date is the break-up date.

Your significant other has just given you a really nice gift. "Here, honey—tickets to the Super Bowl!" On your scheduled break-up date? Thank him or her, take the tickets, proceed as planned.

Times of good news. Your significant other has just received a promotion, gotten a raise, passed the bar. Try not to rain on the parade. But if it's on the appointed break-up date, then move forward. Hey, the good news will help soften the blow.

You've just been caught cheating. Or you're about to cheat. Yep, good time to break up. The sooner the better. Who needs the ugly scene that comes with being discovered? And remember—if you break up before your significant other finds out you've been unfaithful, then it hasn't really been cheating, has it?

Anytime you feel like it. Look, if you find yourself feeling like you can't take it anymore, or suddenly you feel courageous enough to go through with the break-up, then do it right then and there even if it's before the appointed date. Take advantage of your mood to do it. You might feel differently later.

FIVE
Stalker-proof your Break-up

A bad break-up can produce a stalker: an ex who just can't let go or, worse, wants to make you pay for the hurt you've caused. If you're careful and get your ducks properly in a row, you'll be able to avoid the ugly, unnecessary effects that your break-up has the potential to produce. Again, by setting a date in advance and counting the days, you'll have time enough to take care of all the possible contingencies.

Co-worker complications. It's difficult to avoid somebody you've just broken up with if you work together. Rule number one: don't date co-workers. If it happens, make sure you can change the circumstances. Be prepared to transfer to a different department or a different location, even quit and change jobs if you have to. Or else work yourself into a position where you can have your ex transferred. (You'll do it "to help advance" their career, of course.)

Cover your tracks. Does your significant other have something on you? Does he or she know about the drugs you've been dealing or the body buried under the floorboards? Before you leave, make sure that you leave absolutely no incriminating evidence behind.

Do you owe them money? Pay them back. Beg, borrow, or steal if you have to but don't leave your ex with a legal excuse to harass you or take you to small claims court.

Grab your shit. All of it. Make sure everything of yours is out of the house before you leave. Do it while he or she is at work or otherwise not around to see you packing up. Be prepared to kiss goodbye anything that you've forgotten. You don't want to go back and you don't even want to think about what somebody scorned might do with your belongings.

Minimize the collateral damage. Grab the Rolodex that has all of your friends' and family members' phone numbers. Get into your significant other's e-mail program and delete all the e-mail addresses of your friends and family too. Change their phone numbers in your significant other's cell phone. Stalking isn't always done in a direct line. Your scorned ex might decide to stalk you through those you're closest to.

Prepare those around you. Even if you do whatever you can to insulate your friends and family from any collateral damage, it's best to at least give them a heads-up. Let them know in advance about the break-up and make sure they're ready for any unwelcome contact from your ex.

Line up a locksmith. If the break-up means that your significant other is moving out, make sure you get all the locks changed. You don't want to wake up in the middle of the night to see your ex poised over you with a meat cleaver.

Take care of the bills. Do you and your significant other share expenses? Make sure everything is clearly delineated and that your name doesn't appear on the accounts your significant other is responsible for. You don't want unnecessary credit problems.

Leave behind no confidential information. Does your significant other have your social security number written down anywhere? Your driver's license number? Grab any and all records that might otherwise give him or her access to your personal records. Keep your passport and birth certificate in a safe place at all times, away from your significant other, even well before the break-up.

Hide your car. If you don't use your garage this would be a good time to start. If you don't have a garage, park around the corner, out of sight. Flat tires, being keyed, sugar in the gas tank—they might not be able to get to you, but if you're not careful, they'll get to your car.

Internet-proof yourself. Take all necessary precautions if you utilize online communities like Facebook and MySpace. Be prepared for the possibility that your ex might decide to blast you mercilessly in cyber space.

Surprise visits. This is especially problematic at the workplace. If necessary, alert security or at least your receptionist to the idea that your ex might just show up unannounced. Be ready.

SIX
The Aftermath

What happens *after* a break-up—and how you react to what happens—is almost as important as the events leading up to it. Be prepared for these aftermath pitfalls.

Continued communications. It's normally the third day after a break-up that the desperate phone calls, text messages, and e-mails begin. They're too shell-shocked the first day and they're licking their wounds on the second. After that, look out. If you want the communication to stop, you need to be very adamant and firm. I remember in my days as a cop that when somebody was being harassed by endless phone calls from an ex, we were trained to ask, "Did you tell them *very clearly* to stop?" Because if you don't, then you bear some responsibility for them continuing. By not being firm, you've given them a glimmer of hope.

Abuse by proxy. Be prepared that if you don't hear from your ex, you might very well hear from his or her friends. This is especially problematic if they're your friends too. Since you produced the break-up, you'll be regarded as the bad guy. You'll be shunned, cursed at, and generally made to feel like a heel.

Zero sympathy. Even if your friends (or family members) completely understand your reasons for breaking up, they probably still won't understand that *you're* hurt by the experience. Breaking up often hurts the person causing the break-up as much as the other person. Your significant other has become a part of your life. On some level, you're going to miss them.

The pop-in. Chances are good that you *will* see your ex again. They'll surprise you one evening at home, or maybe one day at the office. What are you going to do? You can invite them in, or you can tell them to get lost. The former gives them hope. And who knows? If you miss them as much as they miss you, their visit might lead to something that wasn't exactly on your agenda. Is that necessarily a bad thing? By the time they come around to see you, you might be missing them enough to think the break-up was a mistake. Which leads us to…

The Make-Up. This is a very real possibility. People break up and get back together all the time. Don't be the least bit surprised to discover that you want your ex back in your life. This is a serious matter. Consider carefully the reasons you broke up in the first place. Will those reasons somehow disappear? You don't want to get back together just to break up again a few weeks from now.

Misinterpretations. Even if you don't want to get back with your ex, it's easy sometimes to stay in contact because of guilt feelings you might be harboring. And if you're in communication, it's easy to accidentally say something your ex can misconstrue as a hopeful sign that you want to rekindle the relationship. If you have no intention of rekindling the relationship, this can actually be worse than no communication at all.

Special-Occasion hazards. Months after the break-up your ex sends you a birthday card or a Christmas present, as the case may be. A classy thing to do, or a manipulative attempt at getting back? Trust me: it's the latter.

The trap. It's been awhile and there's been a lot of water under the bridge. Now your ex wants to get back together. Maybe you've decided you want to also. But always remember this: you hurt him or her badly. And revenge is a dish best served cold. Question the motive. Always question the motive.

Stress. Breaking up is stressful. Be prepared for the fact that your attention will be diverted. Your work might suffer. You may not sleep well. You might experience weight gain or loss.

Loss of sex. You've been getting it on a regular basis. Now, with the break-up, it's gone. If you don't already have somebody else in mind to pick up the slack, make sure you've at least stocked up on some serious porn.

Nothing. Nothing might happen afterwards. You might be expecting him or her to come begging. And even if you don't want him or her to do so, and you're relieved that the break is an apparent clean one, it still might be a blow to the ego that you're not being contacted night and day. Count your blessings and move on.

SEVEN
The Dangers of a Substandard Break-up

Doing a poor job at breaking up is a much more serious matter than merely breaching proper etiquette. If you're not careful, you can create a monster. We talked in Chapter Five about practical considerations for stalker-proofing your break-up, but a stalker can be created by more subtle actions—subconscious movements on your part that can backfire and send the exact wrong signal.

Make certain. If you're not 100% sure you want to break up, that's going to become apparent to your significant other who is going to be sitting there desperately grasping at any slim piece of hope you—consciously or subconsciously—toss out to them. If they sense you're not completely serious about the break, they'll keep sticking around.

Promising to stay friends. You're a nice person. You don't want to hurt your significant other's feelings any more than necessary. And so you naturally try to lift their spirits by offering your friendship at least. Bad move. This leaves a door open, producing unwarranted hope. It might be all they need to keep them from going away.

Weak reasoning. If you don't give your significant other a very good reason for wanting to break up, he or she is going to hound you until you do. If you do the Runaway, thus giving no reason at all, you're playing with fire. For a break-up to be truly clean, your ex is going to need some closure.

Poor presentation. Similarly, your reason for breaking up must be delivered in a clear, unequivocal way. There can be no room for hesitation or waffling. Saying things like, "I just want a break…some time for myself" might sound like a break-up to you, but your significant other will take it as a clear invitation to reconvene after a suitable amount of time and pick up right where things were left off. Say exactly what you mean.

Break-up sex. Hey, one more time on the way out the door for old time's sake is okay, isn't it? Just a little something to remember the great times? Wrong. Nothing could be more confusing for your ex.

Responding. To phone calls, e-mails, text messages, or what have you. These are going to be inevitable. We touched on it in the last chapter but it's worth repeating. If you don't want to encourage stalking behavior, you need to be firm about rejecting your ex's communications.

Keeping in regular contact. It's nice of you to send birthday cards and Christmas cards and to keep your ex on your e-mail joke list, and it shows real class on your part. It's also a mixed signal that can become seriously confusing for your ex. "Is he/she still thinking of me?" they'll wonder. And rightfully so.

Kids. If your break-up isn't a divorce and/or the kids aren't yours, then the idea of a clean break applies to them as well. It's not just a bad idea to lead kids on and continue to give them hope where none exists. It's downright cruel.

Look within. Often times people neglect to make a clean break for one simple reason: they're insecure and until somebody else comes along, it's nice to know there's still the ex out there if all else fails. Admit it, it's nice to be mourned over, even stalked. It's flattering. It's also selfish and gutless. If you're determined to move on, then you have to allow your ex to move on too.

EIGHT
The Emergency Break-up

It started with some innocent flirtation. Then there was lunch one day. And although that's where it should have stopped, you agreed to meet for drinks after work a couple days later. Drinks led to dinner. Before you knew what was happening, dinner led to the bedroom. Guess what? You've got yourself a lover on your hands. Good for you, except for one thing: you've already got a significant other someplace else. You try to balance both relationships for as long as you can, but sooner or later you know you can't. You're cheating. More significantly, you realize your new lover is now whom you want to be with. Spending time with your old lover is starting to feel more like cheating than spending time with your new one. Either direction, it's cheating. You have to stop it *now*.

Cover your tracks. The problem with this scenario is two-fold: One—if your soon-to-be-ex realizes that the real reason you're breaking up is because you've been cheating, the break-up and its aftermath are going to be ugly. Two—if your new love ever finds out you were still with somebody else when you met, when you dated, when you made love for the first time; then you're going to be facing a *different* break-up. Plan your strategy—retroactively concoct your timetable to jive with the events as you need them to be perceived. It must always seem as if you broke up with your ex *before* you met your new love.

Enlist friends and family. The only people who might know the real timetable are your friends and family. Time to call in some favors. Everybody has to be on the same page. You don't need your new love talking with some cousin of yours only to hear it revealed unintentionally that there was a little overlap between relationships.

Watch for ex. Popping in, sending cards or gifts, or otherwise keeping in contact. The problem with the overlap scenario is that the break-up is fresh on the ex's mind. And he or she—not knowing the real reason for it—might still be thinking of a reunion. You have to make your break-up especially clear and unmistakable.

Internet Dangers. If you've got a page on an online community then you have to be extra careful what information you post. Otherwise you'll make it way too easy for the ex to see exactly what you're up to and figure out when it all came about. Then you'll have an angry ex on your hands. And that's a recipe for disaster.

Coaching. If the danger exists of your ex continuing to stay in contact, then you have to do some preemptory work. Prepare your new lover by coaching him or her on how unstable your "old" girlfriend/ boyfriend is. "S/he thinks we just broke up, even though it was a year ago! What a nut! Best to just not listen to anything s/he says, darling."

Be prepared. Even with the best laid plans, it could happen. Somebody rats you out, or maybe your new lover puts two and two together all on his or her own, and the next thing you know you're having a confrontation with your ex, your new love, or both. Time to come clean and use the only weapon left in your arsenal: "But I only did it so nobody would get hurt. I only did it out of love."

NINE
Staying Friends

Every now and then, once in a blue moon when all the planets line up perfectly, a couple breaks up amicably and each party still respects the other and still wants to maintain some kind of relationship without any ulterior motive or underlying misconceptions as to the nature of the relationship. Records show that the last time this happened was in June of 1996. But who knows? Maybe your relationship can be the next. If it's possible that you can break up with your significant other and yet remain friends, you might just find yourself in a very special relationship. Some food for thought:

A different perspective. Having somebody of the opposite sex around to bounce ideas off of can be a very valuable thing. If you can get to the point where you feel comfortable asking him or her for relationship advice, you've got yourself a source of insight like no other.

Better friends than lovers. You might find as the relationship develops in its new way that you're now much better together. Some people make better Indians than chiefs and some couples make better friends than lovers.

Never say never. Having an ex-significant other within reach means that the possibility always exists that something might flare up again. This is particularly true if you've broken up more over stage-of-life type differences as opposed to personality conflicts. Sometimes people are just at two different points in their lives, thus making it difficult to keep a relationship together. But then, down the road, the points cross again. It's nice to think that if that happens, your significant other is still around. On the other hand…

No expectations. It's not fair of either party to have unrealistic expectations of where—if anywhere—the friendship might go. If you can't accept the relationship at the friendship level only, then you need to let the relationship go.

No demands. No expectations also means no demands. He or she is just a friend now. If they're dating somebody else, that's entirely their business. You've lost the right to be jealous, angry, or even meddlesome. You have to be big. If you can't be, then you don't deserve the friendship.

Friends with benefits? I don't recommend. Sex confuses things immensely. Then again, sex is sex. And an ex-lover might know what makes the old rocket launch much better than whomever you're currently going out with. It's a judgment call. But proceed with caution.

TEN
Holiday Break-ups

You're either a cheapskate, where you like the idea of breaking up with your significant other before a major holiday so as to save money (only to get back together again after the holiday is safely behind you), or you're afraid of commitment and spending the holidays with your significant other (and family, perhaps) is just too much to even contemplate. Either way, you probably need to do some serious introspection. But that's not my place. I'm not here to judge. If you're intent on scheduling a break-up merely to accommodate your fear of holidays, make sure to do it right.

Think through the pros and cons. Are you sure it's worth it? Yes, you'll save money, but it will be perceived as a selfish act on your part. Then again, in addition to the monetary savings, you'll divest yourself of all the responsibilities that a major holiday entails, which can be quite a relief. But of course you'll have no fond memories of holidays shared with your loved one to look back on. Of course you'll avoid the in-laws which is always nice. But then you'll go down in their minds as being the one that broke things off with their son or daughter or brother or sister right before Christmas or Valentine's Day or their birthday, or whatever the case may be. But at least you'll avoid all the shopping, especially for the Christmas holiday! On the other hand, you'll be leaving your significant other feeling vulnerable and lonely and, perhaps, wanting to seek other company.

Think carefully.

Valentine's Day. If you decide to break up before Valentine's Day, you need to do it no later than, say, the 6th of January to avoid the appearance of wanting to break up *because* of Valentine's Day. By the same token, don't even approach the subject of getting back together until at least February 18th. And to help facilitate the bounce-back, make sure you send your significant other a nice card for V-Day, just to let them know you were thinking of them, even though you were both apart.

Birthday. You need at least a 3-week buffer for the birthday break-up. Break up closer than that to their birthday and they will never forget that you ruined their birthday. And every birthday from then on will present them with a reminder. As with Valentine's Day, send a nice card.

Anniversaries. Here you'll need a month buffer. The anniversary of when you first met or when you first started dating can be an emotional day. But a month beforehand can soften the effects. No greeting card on this one! A Valentine's Day card or a birthday card can be generic. But an anniversary card? When you're broken up? It'll either seem like you've got issues with the break-up, or that you're mocking the relationship.

Christmas. The whole Christmas season is a three-in-one. Play your cards right and you'll avoid Thanksgiving and New Year's, too! The trick is to break up right after Halloween before the season really starts to roll in. A card is nice here, but maybe because of the importance of the season, a well-placed phone call might be well-advised too. The downside to breaking up before the Christmas season? It's a damn long time. Will your significant other still be there after New Year's?

ELEVEN
The Reverse Break-Up

Everyone has one that gets away. Maybe you've discovered you made a mistake by breaking up with your significant other and he or she has become the one, in your life, that got away. Hey, don't beat yourself up about it. Everybody fucks up. And it's probably not too late to fix things. Break-ups don't have to be permanent. They can be reversed, just like vasectomies.

The face to face. You're not going to be able to get back together in an instant. You've hurt this person, remember. It's probably going to be a difficult and lengthy process. You'll need to cajole. You'll need to woo. You'll need to beg. Start with dinner. Make it sound innocent. Meet him or her at a nice restaurant. And be prepared to spend some money. This is no time to split the tab. And do whatever you can to resist being talked into lunch instead of dinner. Lunch is for friends, not lovers.

Don't come empty-handed. When you show up to dinner, come bearing gifts. Flowers for her, a six-pack for him. Stop at Hallmark and grab an apology card. Two of them—one touching and heartfelt, one funny. And dress nice, for cripe's sake. It shows you care. Treat the matter like an interview. Or a first date.

Apologize. This might seem obvious but it's also mandatory. You have to say you're sorry. You have to admit you screwed up. You have to.

Go for the second chance. You need to ask for a second chance before one is granted to you. Be careful with the groveling, though. Nobody respects weakness, especially if you're a guy. She's attracted to you on some level (or was at one time) because she perceives you to be strong. Grovel. But grovel strongly.

Fun, humorous, memorable. These are the qualities you want to shoot for with the please-take-me-back process. Keep it light, keep it fun. Make them feel like a million bucks, and give them some heartfelt words to remember.

Lay it on thick. This is no time to be conservative in your approach. Tell him or her that when you broke up, a piece of you died that day. You no longer feel complete. Say it even if it isn't true. Say *whatever* you need to say, even if it isn't true. A little bullshit never hurts. Sometimes, if you're not lying, it means you're not trying.

Close the sale. In sales we're trained to ask for the order. This is no different. "What's it going to take today to get you back into this relationship?" ABC: *Always Be Closing.*

Expect rejection. It's completely unrealistic to expect him or her to say yes right away. They're going to play hardball. They're going to give you stalls and objections. They'll have ready-made excuses like they've already found someone else. Don't believe it. Keep attacking.

It's a marathon, not a sprint. It's probably going to take more than one dinner. Hell, it might take a hundred dinners. That's okay. You can always go to a secondary plan: ask to simply "maintain the friendship." Keep things innocent and light. But do things together that couples do. Concerts, sporting events, mini-golf. Boyfriend/girlfriend stuff. If you get him or her to keep coming back, you're going to make the sale. In fact, by the end of the third "date," you'll probably be a couple again.

SECTION TWO
So You Just Got Dumped

It happens to all of us. Getting broken up with is as natural a part of life as breathing or eating or picking one's nose. How many days has it been? If you're living in the first couple of days after being dumped, you're living through the toughest part. It gets easier, trust me.

Soon, though, you'll start asking yourself some questions. Some of them you'll answer automatically. Others you'll need to stop and consider. All of them ought to be dealt with at some point, on some level. Here's a preview of the things that may go through your head:

Is it me? Is it something I did or didn't do?
Is it physical? Am I good-looking enough?
What was it that I did that pushed this person into a gay lifestyle?

Is life worth living, or should I off myself right now?
Is it at all possible that I can find the solace I'm seeking in junk food?

How about drugs and/or alcohol?
How about I get another credit card and start down the long road to recovery by indulging my desire to go shopping?

Listening repeatedly to sad music and/or "our song": Good idea or bad?

Should I delete his or her number from my cell phone?
How soon do I start dating again?
Is it okay if I *never* date again?

Should I seek professional help?
Should I continue to stay in shape, or let myself go entirely to shit?

Let's look a little closer at this whole getting dumped thing. Sure, there's a lot on your mind right now. And it can be overwhelming. But that's why I'm here. Let's see if we can get all this sorted out and help you make sense of your life again.

TWELVE
Day 1

You're numb. You're a deer in headlights. You're thinking back to the events of yesterday and you're saying, "What—for crying out loud—*just happened!?* Well stop it. Pull yourself together. Don't sit there feeling sorry for yourself. Pick yourself up off the floor.

Start dating. What?! The day after you were just dumped? You bet your ass. And in this day and age it's easy to do. Go online to a dating site and fill out a profile. Now.

Exaggerate. While you're filling out that profile, don't be afraid to…shall we say, bend the truth a little? Look, right now you need to give yourself a shot of confidence. The best, quickest way to do so is to give yourself an image to live up to. Describe yourself in the best terms possible. At this point it's all about self-image. Make it a great one.

Shop around. And while you're building yourself up to the world, go ahead and look at some of the other profiles. Guess what? There are *a lot* of single people out there. When you get dumped you have a tendency to feel isolated and cut off from the rest of the world, as though the rest of the world is made up of nothing but happy, smiling, loving couples. Nope. Most people are just like you.

Take care of yourself. During Day 1 your shell-shock is causing you to ignore your basic self-grooming routine. You don't want to shower, you don't want to shave, you don't want to put on any make-up. You're thinking, what's the point? But it's important that you take care of your appearance. Trust me. You'll feel better about yourself and if you feel better about yourself, you'll feel better about the world.

Move your ass. Get up. Get going. You want to sit there like a lump, but that's self-defeating. Go to work, go shopping, go fishing. Make it business as usual. But isn't that denying your true feelings? you ask. Shouldn't you take some time to mourn? Sounds like somebody's been watching too much Oprah. You can wallow in the touchy-feely crap, if you like. I'm more interested in doing what it takes to get on with life.

Have sex! There's nothing better than releasing your tension and stress with a nice little sexual tryst. It'll give you a much-needed boost. Unfortunately, your latest source of bedroom fun just dumped you. What now? Two words: self gratification. "Don't knock masturbation," Woody Allen once said. "It's having sex with someone I love."

Eat. You need your strength. Eat a healthy meal. You might not be hungry, but force it down. No ice cream binges! And no fast food. You need good, energy-producing fare. It'll get you through Day 1 and send you feeling much better into…

THIRTEEN
Day 2

Your shock has now turned to hate. Well, that's progress I guess. At least you're more energetic. It's just that your energy is wrongly directed. You need to get on with life, and hating the person who just dumped you, or hating "all men" or "all women", or hating the entire world for your problems, isn't going to help you do that.

It's *your* life. First, realize this. Don't let anybody rent space in your brain. If you can't rid yourself of thoughts about the person who just walked out of your life, then you're allowing them to take over. And don't assume they're coming back. There's nothing for you to wait for. It's time to move on. Now.

Get rid of their stuff. You don't need their crap in your house. Toss whatever they've left behind.

Destroy all photos. From the ones hanging on the walls to the ones in your cell phone. Pictures of your ex will only serve as hurtful reminders.

Toss the gifts. Every gift they gave you will remind you of a special occasion. Dump 'em. Or sell them. Or re-gift them. Just get them out of the house.

No revenge! Your hatred is causing you to think of all the cruel and wonderful things you can do to "get even" with the offending jerk/bitch. Stop it. Do you really want to confirm in his or her mind that breaking up with you was the right thing to do? The best revenge is a life well-lived. Start living.

Minimize the stress. Keep the anxiety at bay. Do a low-impact workout. Walk around the block a few times. Take the edge off. Two words: self gratification.

Get out of the house tonight. Do yourself a favor and go out tonight. But no drinking! You're not ready for that yet. All drinking is likely to do is make you obsess about your situation. Keep a clear head. Who knows? Maybe you'll find someone. You don't want a rebound relationship, though. Just go for some quick, no-obligation sympathy sex.

Brain scrub. Fill your mind with anything and everything besides thoughts of your ex. This will get easier as the days come and go. For now it will be a chore to focus your thoughts elsewhere, but focus elsewhere you must.

FOURTEEN
Day 3

By now your anger and hatred are hopefully subsiding. Unfortunately, you might find yourself instead preoccupied with thoughts about how to get your lover back. Wrong thoughts. You need to be thinking about how to get *you* back. This is a day of introspection and serious self-appraisal. Did you get the "it's not you, it's me," line? Well we know from Part I that that was a lie. Sorry. It *is* you. Let's find out why.

Stepped on a scale lately? 38% of break-ups occur because one party has become disgusted with the other party's consistent weight gain. Okay, I just made that statistic up. But it doesn't hurt to consider the fact that maybe, over time, you had started to become less and less physically attractive to your partner.

Unhappiness is contagious. Is it possible that your partner left you because he or she just couldn't take continually being dragged down into the depths of your depression and gloom? Nobody wants to be with somebody who's always in a bad mood. And, no, it's not their job to put you in a good mood. You need to find happiness within. In fact, that's the only place you can find it.

Narcissism. Things are not always about you, you know. Start making notes of how many times you use the word "I" in a typical conversation. Learn what the words "sympathy" and "empathy" mean.

Predictability. Are you boring? Do you lack a certain sense of adventure and impulsiveness? Then it's time to get a tattoo and start sporting an earring.

Unpredictability. Maybe you have the opposite problem: impulsiveness. Wildness and recklessness can seem an awful lot like irresponsibility.

Lousy lover. This is nothing to be ashamed of. Not everybody can have the skill, stamina, or dexterity of a porn star. It's tempting to want to read a manual and learn some fancy techniques. Mistake. Keep it simple. Take your time, be attentive to your lover's needs, seek to please. That's all there is to it.

Make-over. You know, if all else fails, maybe you just need a new *you*. New wardrobe, new hairdo, new look. Hell, acquire a new walk even. Be different. Be bold. Reinvent yourself. Now's the time.

Status quo. Or, it might be possible that there's not a damn thing wrong with you. But you can only come to this conclusion if you have been brutally honest with yourself. Have you? Probably not, but if so, then maybe all you need to change is your taste in members of the opposite sex. Find somebody who's going to appreciate you for you, unlike the clueless loser who just broke up with you.

FIFTEEN
Day 4

It's time to get back on the horse. We touched on dating back on Day 1, but now it's time to get serious.

Go online. Did you take my advice back on Day 1 to set up a profile on a dating site? You should have. (Would I steer you wrong?) If not, do it now. We have the luxury of living in the best possible time the world has ever known for finding somebody. We live in the technology, information age. There's *nothing* you can't find online.

It's a numbers game. Ask out as many people as possible. If you have to ask one-hundred people out to get one date, then ask one-hundred people out. Ask two-hundred. Or three-hundred. You'll gain confidence just by the act of asking. And confidence is appealing. For both men and women. People have this erroneous idea that men are intimidated by strong, confident women. Bullshit. We love 'em.

It's a numbers game Part II. Go out with as many people as possible. Even if you're not sure you want to spend an evening with any given person, go ahead and do it if for no other reason than to benefit yourself by the simple practice of dating. Plus, you just never know: maybe after spending an evening with somebody you didn't fine appealing right off the bat, you might discover something surprising. Turning down a chance to go out on a date with somebody is like turning down a job interview before you even know what the job pays.

Go out with them twice. This is an extension of #3. Unless it's a complete, unmitigated disaster, you shouldn't judge the possibilities of a potential relationship by the first date alone.

It's dating, not sex. It's tempting to want to get some of what you've been missing since your ex left. But we're not rebounding for sex. We're rebounding to rebuild what's been damaged. This isn't a sex issue, this is a self-esteem issue. Sex is going to confuse things. Can't wait? Two words: self gratification.

And while we're on the subject of rebounding…Don't think of it as such. You're in for minor repairs; you're looking to patch up a few leaks. Rebounding is desperate. Rebounding is grabbing the first thing that comes along like it's a life preserver to a drowning man. This is *not* an attractive condition. And other people can sense it, especially women who have an uncanny knack for identifying desperation and running from it.

Friends. If you haven't already told every friend and acquaintance you have that you're back on the market, do so before this day ends. Somebody somewhere knows of somebody who's just right for you.

SIXTEEN
Day 5

Let's face it. You haven't really been paying much attention to this section of the book, have you? You're still feeling sorry for yourself, you vacillate between hating your ex and missing him or her terribly (either way he or she is all you're thinking about), you haven't stopped for one moment for any serious self-reflection, and you have zero plans to get back into the dating world. If you're not careful, your obsession is going to take a nasty turn into stalking behavior. Nip it.

No communication. Phone calls, e-mails, text messages. Even if it's something you would normally do. After all, you're thinking, s/he's on my e-mail list anyway, right? And so you forward an e-mail out to everybody with the joke of the day. C'mon. Be honest with yourself. It was probably a stupid joke that you would otherwise not in a million years forward, but you just wanted your ex to see your name pop up in his or her inbox. Stop it.

No "friends". Your ex broke up with you so why do you still have them listed under "friends" on your online community page? Sorry, but they no longer belong there.

No gifts, no cards. I know it's his or her birthday. So what? They dumped you. They don't get a card.

No drive-by's. He or she is *not* on your way home, so why do you keep driving by their place? To see if they're home. To see if somebody else's car is there. To see if maybe they're standing in the front yard just waiting to take you back. (They're not). All terrible reasons.

No accidental calls. Oops, you misdialed. You meant to speed-dial somebody else but hit your ex's number instead. Please. Jung said there are no accidents and he was right.

No chance meetings. You know he or she goes to happy hour after work on every single Tuesday at the exact same place. And yet you "just happen" to show up there. Guess what that makes you? (Hint: it rhymes with "walker.")

No pics. I once broke up with a girl who continued to have my picture on her Facebook page as well as her laptop's screen saver. *Two years later*. That's not stalking—that's psychotic.

Stop talking! Your friends and family have been wonderful at listening to your tales of misery and woe. The problem is, you just keep talking about it. It's good to get things off your chest, but c'mon. Enough is enough. Move on, if for no other reason than to preserve the sanity of your loved ones.

SEVENTEEN
Day 6

Maybe it doesn't happen Day 6. Maybe it doesn't happen until day 60, or 600. But sooner or later it's going to happen. The world isn't that big. You're going to bump into your ex somewhere. Are you ready?

Talk yourself up. Nothing is going to make you feel better than letting your ex know how great you're getting along without him or her. Even if it's not true. The last thing you need is pity from the ex. That's a hole too deep to even contemplate. "You were right to break up with me," you say. "We clearly don't belong together and the break-up has actually been the best, most healthy thing ever for me. Thanks!"

Make mention of your new love. Even if you don't have one. Might as well get a little satisfaction from rubbing it in. Nothing obvious, mind you. Just a brief mention of the football player or Victoria's Secret model you've been dating lately.

Keep in shape, look your best. Always, because you never know when that chance meeting is going to occur.

Look virtually good, too. Update your online community page. Your ex might be curious. If you haven't already done so, take his or her picture down. Talk about all the great things you're doing—your trip to

Paris, your Mediterranean cruise, your impending nomination to the Supreme Court and your Academy Award for Best Director.

Give 'em the cold shoulder. You'll be having a great time, when you bump into them, telling all about the wonderful things you're now doing with your life. But pause for a second and ask them how *they're* doing. Wait until they're about three seconds into their answer and hit 'em with this: "Oh, wow, is that the right time?" (looking at your watch). "I'm sorry, I really have to get going. I told the guy at the Masarati dealership I'd be picking up my car this afternoon. Bye for now! Great seeing you!"

Be ready. They're going to want you back. And rejecting them is the best closure of all. And even if they never want you back, isn't it better to continue through life with some pride, without having your ex feeling sorry for you?

EIGHTEEN
Day 7

And on the seventh day, ye shall rest. Well, not really. You need to get out into the world and get past your heartbreak. But maybe we can at least make things easier today by simplifying. Here's a quick and easy list of Do's and Don'ts.

Do have an outlet. You need to blow off steam, or at least have something that serves as a decent substitute for what you're now missing since the big dump. Sure it's not healthy in excess, or for long periods, but if you're going to spend any time in your life smoking or drinking (or both) now would probably be the best time.

Do keep a journal. Have a place where you can write your thoughts—all of them. The negative ones, the ugly ones, the dangerous ones—leave nothing out. It'll give you a means by which to verbalize what's going on in your head, a place to export all of the negativity. It's also a good place to write down some short-term goals, maybe ways to improve yourself or ways to get out of your funk. A journal can be like a friend you confide in, except that unlike your real friends, it never gets bored or stops listening.

Do exercise. It's good for the body as well as for the mind.

Do eat well. You need to keep your strength. If you start to ignore yourself physically, your mental well-being will follow.

Do take some sort of stimulant. Hey I'm not advocating drug usage, but an energy drink or two might not hurt. A little caffeine or something to put a little pep in your step might just help you get moving.

Don't overeat. I said eat well, not eat like a pig. It's easy to want to take refuge in food, but a heavy meal will bring you down. And eating a ton right before you go to bed is even worse. You'll sleep poorly, put on weight, and feel like crap.

Don't under eat. This is almost as bad as overeating. People tend to go one way or the other on this. If they're not seeking refuge in comfort food, then their appetite is gone completely and they can't bring themselves to eat anything at all.

Don't be negative. This brings you and everybody else around you down. And strangers—potential new lovers, for example—sense it. Nobody wants to hang around a cynic.

Don't be hateful. Sure, you're still pissed off at your ex. But if you don't let it go, it will not only turn you into a stalker, it'll affect every future relationship.

NINETEEN
Day 8

It's probably too optimistic by Day 8 to imagine that you're now seeing that the break-up was a good thing. But the truth is that all things happen for a reason. Someday you'll look back at being dumped and realize it was the best thing that could have happened. Why?

Because s/he was the wrong one. Maybe this has thus far escaped you because it's *too* obvious: if your ex was the right person for you, *they'd still be with you.* But they're not. Therefore...? Surely you can solve this little logic puzzle, even in your depressed state of mind.

Because you'll find someone better. A corollary to the above. Since we've determined your ex is not right for you, it stands to reason that without the break-up, you might have never been given a chance to find the one who is. He or she is out there somewhere, and you're now free to look.

Because you can become a better person. The break-up gives you the opportunity to do some serious soul-searching. This is *always* a good thing.

Because you can become a stronger person. Nietzsche said that that which does not kill us makes us stronger. You will become stronger by this experience.

Because the load is now off. Sometimes people don't fully realize how weighed down they are with somebody until they break up with them. You're free now. You can do what you want. You can start your life all over again. You can be who you want to be. Go where you want to go. See who you want to see. The opportunities boggle the mind. You're limited now only by your imagination. Congratulations as you make your way back out into the world, a world which is now at your fingertips.

TWENTY
And in Conclusion…

Maybe you're the dumper. Maybe you're the dumpee. Neither side is without its difficulties. Then again, neither side is without its share of life lessons. No matter what your role in a break-up, you're going to learn much from the experience. It's not always easy, but that's the way it seems to be with life lessons. They're often painful and challenging. There are a few things that will stand out more than others, though. Things that are almost universal to all break-ups. Things of which you'll want to be especially aware:

The break-up to make-up. This happens. A lot. People break-up and suddenly realize what they're missing. I'm not saying your break-up is necessarily going to result in you getting back together with your ex, but I am saying that the experience often leads to a re-examination of things. It's only natural, and something you'll need to anticipate.

Sex confuses things. I've said it before but it bears repeating. A lot of break-ups (and make-ups) take place under the cloud of sexual confusion. Lust ends up ruling the day and decisions get made that aren't necessarily based on any kind of intellectual process. Watch out. That's all I'm saying.

Stay out of the friend's zone. [Jim, I didn't write up anything for this one because I'm wondering if we should leave it out. We've got an entire chapter (9) dedicated to some of the advantages of staying friends and this seems contradictory. What do you think? I can write something up if you want me to.]

Being a cheater. Look, if you're a serial cheater, then you just need to come to grips with that. You need to be mature and admit it. Be a dater. But don't bother to get into serious relationships where you're breaking up with people every other week because they've either discovered you're cheating, or you've discovered someone better in the course of your cheating.

Dating a cheater. Don't. Learn to identify a player when you see one. And don't think you're the one person in the world who can change him or her. You can't.

Strive for a little unpredictability. One of the life lessons you might learn from being dumped is that maybe you need to change things up a bit. Be a little different, try some new things. It will help you grow, and it might even make you more attractive. On the other hand…

Be yourself. Don't change your life just to suit others. Do it for your own purposes of growth and development. Trying to be somebody you're not isn't very attractive anyway. If somebody wants a different you, then they might be better served looking for somebody else to begin with.

Enjoy being single. You know, in all the consternation and pain of being dumped, you might have overlooked something. Being single can be wonderful. You can go where you want to go, do what you want to do, be who you want to be. It's a time of growth and opportunity, a time of self-reflection, a time to get to know who you really are. You might learn to like it so much that you'll only be willing to give it up for somebody really, really, really, really special. And of course that's exactly as it should be.

Self-examination. Whether you're the dumper or the one dumped, this is a good time to sit back and reflect on what happened and what the situation says about *you*. You might learn more about yourself from this break-up than from anything else that's happened to you or is going to happen to you.

Fear of commitment. In the course of your self-examination, take a look at this little pest. You might have dumped somebody for no better reason than your fear of commitment. Or, your fear might have provoked somebody to have broken up with *you*. Either way, you might want to address it. Unless of course you're fine with the pattern of falling in love repeatedly and breaking up every time.

The happy ending. Most of the time there isn't one. This isn't Hollywood, this is real life. Break-ups happen. People get hurt all the time. Relationships are hard work and there are no guarantees even in the best of circumstances. The point is, you need to learn to deal with the reality and not spend your time…

Feeling sorry for yourself. No good. Ever. No "woe is me" crap. Cut it out.

The grass is always greener. No it's not. If you're breaking up repeatedly because your head keeps getting turned by potential lovers you imagine to be better than the one you're with, always remember this truism: no matter how hot s/he is, somebody, somewhere, is sick of his/her shit.

Cupid's arrow. You can't escape it. You're going to meet people, date people, fall in love, have relationships, break up, make up, and do it all over again. They call it life, and you might as well say 'yes' to it. The trick is to take each experience and come away just a little wiser than before. If you can do that, you'll be doing it right.